I WANT

...That every parent holds hidden thoughts in their heart, unspoken words that linger, waiting for the right moment.

These are emotions that cannot be explained by simple reason, the ones that flow through the days, that grow with you, that accompany you as you learn to live. In this book, there are only a few of these words. Words born from the purest love, from pride, from hope, from fear.

Words that tell of the beauty of being a parent, but also the greatness of being a child.

Every thought within these pages is a small part of a bond that knows no boundaries, no time. A bond that feeds on every gesture, every glance, every step you take.
A bond that endures everything, that grows and transforms with you.

These words are my gift to you, a story of emotions, dreams, and memories that you can read and reread.
Every blank space I've filled for you adds a piece of history, a piece of my heart.

Because our story, the story no one else knows...
is the most beautiful of all.

Every day I spend by your side is a life lesson. You are not only my greatest joy but also my inspiration.

Watching you grow, discovering the world with those eyes full of wonder, reminds me that life is made of small magical moments.

If I could go back, there are so many things I would do differently... but you know what? I wouldn't change ANYTHING that led me to you. Because you are my chance to do everything better.

I promise I will always be here to guide you, to support you, to teach you not to fear chasing your dreams, to believe in yourself even when the world feels like a hard place.

You are my future, my heart, and the reason I want to be a better person every day.

I LOVE YOU more than words can ever explain, and I can't wait to see all the wonders you will create in your life.

I WISH TO TELL YOU HOW I FELT WHEN I FOUND OUT
I WAS GOING TO BECOME A PARENT.

The day you were born, time stood still.

I still remember how everything froze, even my breath, the first time I saw you..

A overwhelming mix of emotions flooded over me: the uncontrollable joy of finally meeting you, the fear of not being enough to protect you from everything, and the wonder of knowing that within me was born a love so great it couldn't be measured.

I looked at you, tiny and perfect, and felt the sweet weight of the responsibilities you carried with you: the desire to give you everything you would ever need, to teach you to be strong, kind, and free.

In that moment, I realized I would never be the same person again. Every dream, every fear, every hope I had, was now contained in you.

That day wasn't just your birth, it was mine too: as a parent, as a new person, as someone who found a greater purpose than themselves.

And while the world kept moving on, I stayed there, with you in my arms, silently promising you that I would always do my best to deserve the honor of belonging to you.

I WANT TO TELL YOU WHAT I FELT WHEN I FOUND OUT I WAS GOING TO BE A PARENT

Every time I look at you, I wonder
what kind of person you will see in me.

I don't want to be perfect, because I
know I'm not, but I want to be real.

I want to teach you to be brave, not
with words, but with actions.

I want you to see in me someone who
falls and gets back up, someone who
faces their fears.

Because I know that one day, you will
do the same.

And even though I often hide the
weight of inadequacy, it drives me to
know that every step I take is a lesson
you might carry with you.

I WANT TO TELL YOU WHAT I FELT ON THE DAY YOU WERE BORN.

No matter how hard it gets, how tired I
am, or how many mistakes I make.

I will ALWAYS love you,
unconditionally, without limits,
without needing any explanation.

The love I feel for you asks for nothing
in return, because it has existed since
the moment you took your first breath.

And it is so strong, so immense, that I
wonder how it is even possible to hold
it all.

Even on the darkest days, even when I
am far away, know that my love will be
the invisible thread that keeps you
close to me, wherever you go.

I WANT YOU TO KNOW HOW DIFFERENT THE
WORLD WAS THE DAY YOU WERE BORN.

I watch you grow and I can't stop
time.

Every day I see in you a step
forward, a new discovery, a piece of
childhood slipping away.

It's a sweet melancholy, a selfish
desire to keep you small, to protect
you from everything.

But I know my job is not to hold
you back, but to let you go, slowly,
to see who you will become.

Every moment that passes is a gift,
and I cherish every smile of yours,
every word, as if it were eternal.

I WANT TO TELL YOU WHAT IT FELT LIKE TO HEAR YOU SAY YOUR FIRST WORD.

Your first times are also mine. The first smile, the first step, the first word: each moment is a discovery that takes my breath away.

You teach me that every small achievement is a huge milestone, and that happiness hides right there, in the first uncertain steps toward something new.

Every time I see the world through your eyes, it's as if I'm discovering it for the first time too.

And you remind me that we never stop learning, growing, or living.

I WANT TO TELL YOU ABOUT THE FIRST LITTLE GIFT I GAVE YOU.

I remember perfectly the day I took you to your first day of school.

My heart was pounding, but I tried not to let you see my emotion.
I wanted you to be happy, excited, ready to discover the world that was waiting for you.

And yet, as I watched you walk into that school, with your backpack that seemed almost too big for you, I felt the weight of a moment that would change everything.

That moment marked the beginning of a new chapter, one in which you would begin to build your independence, have new experiences, and grow.

I want you to know that even though my heart tightened a little in that moment, I was incredibly PROUD of you.

And somehow, even though we were apart for a while, I was still with you, in every step you took, in every new discovery.

Because no matter where I go, I will always be with you, in your heart, as you learn to walk on your own.

I WANT TO TELL YOU WHAT THE FIRST WORDS
WERE THAT I USED TO DESCRIBE YOU TO OTHERS.

Being a parent means living
with a piece of your heart
walking outside of your body.

Every day, I face the fear of not
doing enough, of not being
enough.

I wonder if I'm making the
right decisions, if I'll know how
to protect you, if the world will
be kind to you.

But then I remember that I
don't have to be perfect, I just
have to be there.

To be your shelter, your guide,
your steady point.

And I hope that, even with my
limits, you will always know
how much you are loved.

I WANT YOU TO KNOW HOW I CHOSE YOUR NAME AND WHY I CONSIDER IT SPECIAL

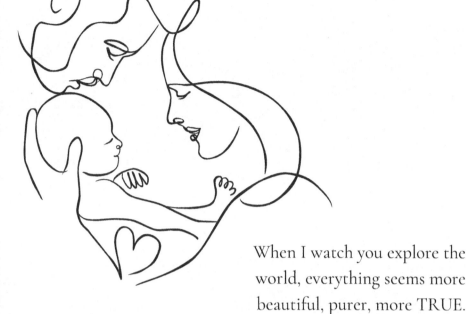

When I watch you explore the
world, everything seems more
beautiful, purer, more TRUE.

Every leaf, every sound, every
discovery becomes an adventure.
You teach me to slow down, to see
the beauty I've forgotten

.

You see the world without filters,
with that curiosity that transforms
the ordinary into the extraordinary.

And thanks to you, I am learning to
do it again.
You are my mirror, my reminder
that life is full of wonders, you just
have to stop and look.

I WANT TO DESCRIBE WHAT YOU WERE LIKE AS A CHILD.

I held you in my arms and felt
the sweet weight of
everything you are.

Every day, I asked myself how
to help you grow, how to
teach you to believe in
yourself, to never stop
dreaming.

It's an immense
responsibility, but also the
greatest gift of my life.

The funny thing, though, is
that all of this, you taught me.

I WANT YOU TO KNOW HOW I FELT WHEN I SAW
YOU TAKE YOUR FIRST STEP.

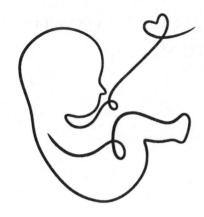

You've changed me in ways I
never thought were possible.

You've taught me patience,
strength, and the
importance of being present.

You've shown me the world
through new eyes, made me
rediscover the joy in the
little things.

Being your parent is the
most challenging journey,
but also the most beautiful
one I could ever undertake.

THANKS to you, I've
become a better version of
myself.

I WANT YOU TO KNOW HOW MUCH I'VE CHANGED
SINCE YOU CAME INTO MY LIFE.

When I think about your future,
my heart fills with hope.

I don't know where life will take
you, what challenges you'll face, or
what dreams you'll follow, but I
know I will always be here to
support you.

I want you to grow knowing that
you can become whoever you
want, that you have everything
inside you to make the world a
better place.

Your future is a blank page, and I
can't wait to see the beautiful
colors with which you will fill it.

I WANT YOU TO KNOW WHAT I FELT ON YOUR FIRST DAY OF SCHOOL.

Before you, life was different.

Simpler, perhaps, but less rich. Since you arrived, every day has a new meaning.

Your presence has transformed my existence, filling the empty spaces I didn't even know I had.

I can't even remember what life was like without you, and I wouldn't go back for anything in the world.

Because you are my reason, my joy, my EVERYTHING.

I WANT TO TELL YOU ABOUT A FUNNY THING THAT
HAPPENED WHEN YOU WERE LITTLE.

I've never said it in words, but every hug, every caress, every smile is a promise.

I promise to always be there for you, to love you without reservation, to support you in every step you take.

I promise to protect you, but also to let you fall, because that's how you will learn to rise again.

I promise to believe in you, even when you don't.

Because my greatest promise is that I will be your shelter, forever.

I WANT YOU TO KNOW WHAT IT MEANS TO ME TO
SEE YOU SMILE.

There are moments when you look at me with eyes that seem like mine.

A gesture, a smile, an expression: I recognize myself in you, and I see myself reflected in you.

It's a deep connection, something that goes beyond words.

It reminds me that we're not separate, that your story runs through mine like a thread.

And in those moments, I feel part of something eternal, something that will never end.

I WANT YOU TO KNOW WHAT SCARED ME THE
MOST WHEN YOU CAME INTO MY LIFE.

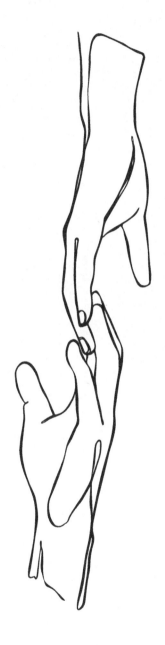

Every moment we live together is a piece of history that I will treasure forever.

I want you to remember our hugs, the laughter, the stories I tell you before bed.

I want you to have a treasure chest of memories full of love, because one day, it will be those memories that will make you feel safe, even when I am far away.

Every day, I build with you a piece of that treasure, and I do it with all my HEART.

I WANT TO TELL YOU WHAT YOUR ROOM WAS LIKE
WHEN WE PREPARED IT TOGETHER FOR
THE FIRST TIME.

Thank you.

Thank you for teaching me what it truly means to love.

Thank you for the smiles you give me every day, for the lessons you teach me without even knowing it.

Thank you for choosing me as your parent.

Every day I spend with you is a gift, and I never take it for granted.

You've changed me, you've made me better, and for that, I will be forever grateful.

I WANT YOU TO KNOW WHAT IT WAS LIKE TO SEE
YOU FACE YOUR FIRST CHALLENGE.

There are days when I wonder if I'm truly showing you the right path, if the choices I make today will be the ones you'll remember tomorrow.

Being a parent isn't about giving answers, but teaching you how to seek them.

I want you to know that, even when you're lost, the compass I am trying to build inside of you will always bring you back to your heart. It's in there that you'll find the courage, strength, and truth of who you are.

And even when you're far away, know that a part of me will always walk beside you.

"I'D LIKE TO TELL YOU ABOUT THE MOMENTS THAT
MADE ME FEEL MOST PROUD OF YOU."

My biggest dream for you is not that you follow in my footsteps, but that you find the courage to create your own.

I want you to know that you should never change to please anyone, that the value of your life lies in your authenticity.

Being yourself is your greatest strength. If you look at yourself in the mirror and see a free and sincere person, I will know I've done something right.

There is no greater gift than seeing you grow into who you truly are.

I WANT YOU TO KNOW WHAT MAKES ME HAPPIEST
WHEN WE'RE TOGETHER.

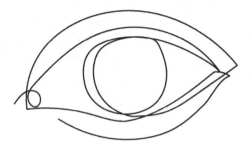

There will be a day when I will watch
you leave, ready for your journey.

And even though my heart will ache, I
will be there, smiling at you with pride.
I will let you go not because I want to,
but because it's right for you to
discover the world with your own eyes.

But know that the door of our home
will always be open, and the arms that
raised you will always be ready to hold
you.

No matter how far you go, no matter
how much you change: to me, you will
always be my miracle.

I WANT TO DESCRIBE A DAY SPENT WITH YOU THAT
HAS STAYED IN MY HEART.

There are things I can't tell
you in words, because they
seem too big to be spoken.

They are the emotions that
hide in gestures: a hand on
your shoulder, a hug before
you even notice, a look that
says 'I'm here for you'.

Even when I can't find the
words, I want you to know
that in every silence there is
love, in every gesture there
is a promise: the promise to
never leave you alone, to
always be your anchor.

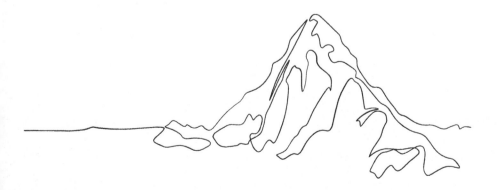

I WANT YOU TO KNOW HOW I IMAGINE OUR BOND
IN A FEW YEARS.

I can't promise you an easy life, because I know that challenges are part of the journey.

But I can promise you that it will be a full life, if you're willing to chase what you love with all of yourself.

Happiness doesn't come without effort, but its value is in the journey itself. I want to teach you that it's worth falling, getting back up, and fighting for what truly matters.

And as you build your path, I will always be here to support you, to cheer you on, and to remind you of your worth.

I WANT YOU TO KNOW WHAT MAKES ME SMILE
WHEN I THINK OF YOU.

Every decision I make
carries your reflection.

There isn't a day that goes
by when I don't ask myself
if I'm doing enough, if I'm
building a world you
deserve.

I want to leave you
something that lasts
beyond time: not material
things, but the memory of
someone who loved you
without reservations, the
value of what is right, the
strength to always choose
with your heart.

My choices today will be
your roots tomorrow.

I WISH YOU KNEW HOW I FELT THE MOMENT I
REALIZED YOU WERE NO LONGER A CHILD.

When you came into my
life, I thought it was my job
to teach you everything.
But the truth is, we are
growing together.

Every day, you show me
things I've never noticed,
teaching me to see the
world with new eyes.

You're learning to walk,
and I'm learning to guide
you; you're discovering
words, and I'm learning to
choose the right ones.

Growing together means
accepting that I will never
be perfect, but I will always
do my best to be worthy of
your love.

I WANT YOU TO KNOW WHAT I WISH FOR YOU IN LIFE.

I will never be the perfect
parent, and you know what?

That's okay.

I want you to see my mistakes
too, because it's from them that
you'll learn that no one is
invincible.

It's in the falls that we find the
greatest lessons, and I want to
show you that it's okay to make
mistakes, that true courage lies
in getting back up.

The love I have for you doesn't
depend on perfection, nor will
your happiness depend on it.

You are already enough, just as
you are.

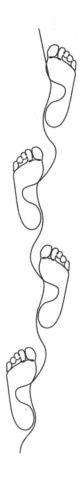

I WANT YOU TO KNOW HOW I FEEL EVERY TIME YOU
TELL ME YOU NEED ME.

There are days that seem to pass in the blink of an eye, but inside, I carry them all with me.

Every laugh, every tear, every hug is a memory I hold close, even when time seems to erase them.

One day, when you're grown and the world feels too fast, I hope you can stop and remember these moments.

Because, even when time slips away, the love that created them stays forever.

I WANT TO TELL YOU WHAT I DID TO HELP YOU
FALL ASLEEP WHEN YOU WERE A CHILD.

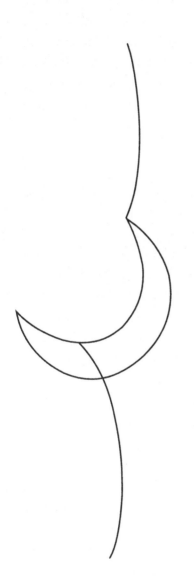

Never stop dreaming,
even when the world
tells you that you can't
make it.

Dreams are the engine
that will take you
wherever you want to
go.

If there's one thing I
want to teach you, it's
that true strength lies in
believing in yourself.

It doesn't matter how
big or crazy your dream
may seem: if you truly
desire it, you can make
it a reality.

And I will always be
there, cheering you on.

I WOULD LIKE TO TELL YOU WHAT I WOULD DO DIFFERENTLY, IF I COULD GO BACK.

The world can be tough, I know.

But I want you to remember that you
will always have a safe haven in me.

When life feels scary, when you feel
lost or alone, I will be here, ready to
hold you just like I did the very first
time.

No matter how many years pass, no
matter how much you change: home
isn't a place, it's the love that
connects us.

I WANT TO TELL YOU ABOUT A CHRISTMAS EVE WE SPENT TOGETHER, ONE THAT I HOLD DEAR IN MY HEART.

There are dreams I've let go of
to walk alongside you, and
you know what?

I don't regret them. Because
now, your dreams have
become mine.

Every victory you achieve,
every milestone you reach,
every smile you wear is my
new purpose.

There's no greater happiness
than watching you
accomplish what you love.

And as you chase your
dreams, remember this: I'll
always be right there, behind
you, cheering you on, every
step of the way.

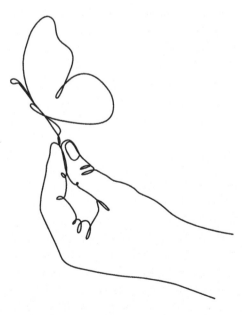

I WANT TO TELL YOU ABOUT ONE OF THE
MISCHIEFS YOU GOT UP TO AS A CHILD.

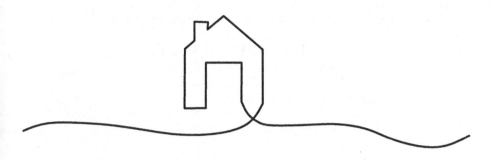

When I look at you, I see
the future.

I see everything you could
become, everything you
already are.

In your eyes, there's a
light that reminds me the
world is full of
possibilities, that every
day is a new chance to
grow, to love, to learn.

Never lose that light,
because it's what makes
you unique, what will
make you an
extraordinary person.

I WANT TO TELL YOU ABOUT OUR
FIRST TRIP TOGETHER.

One day, as I looked at you, I realized that everything in life has a purpose.

You are my beginning and my future, the reason why every challenge is worth it.

The circle of life finds its meaning in the moment you understand that everything you give will come back in ways you could never imagine.

And I will never stop giving you love, hope, and dreams, because I know all of it will live on in you - and beyond me.

I WOULD LIKE TO TELL YOU WHAT I FELT WHEN I LOOKED AT YOUR SCHOOL MARKS.

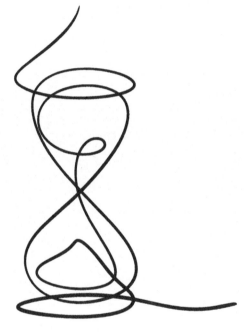

The time is a gentle thief.

It will steal away your tiny hands in mine, those wobbly steps toward me, and even the sound of your childlike laughter that fills the house.

But it can never take you away from my heart.
No matter how much you grow, how far you go, or how the world shapes you, in my eyes, you will always be my child.

I watched you come into this world with the strength of a miracle, and I will never stop seeing you with that same wonder, even when you're all grown up.

I will always be here, with the same strength and love as before, because the one thing time can never touch is the bond between us.

I WANT TO TELL YOU HOW GOOD YOU ARE AT...

There are days when I stop and think about how much you've changed.

Every day, you become a little more independent, a little older, and while that fills me with pride, it also makes me feel nostalgic at times.

I think about all the times I held you in my arms, when I was your whole world.

Now, your world is expanding, filled with people, experiences, and choices that are all your own.

Yet, even though your journey will take you far from me, I want you to know one thing: I will always be here.

I WOULD LIKE TO TELL YOU WHAT I BELIEVE ARE
YOUR GREATEST QUALITIES.

I don't know if one day you'll be able to understand how important you've been to me. Before you, I thought I knew what love was.

I thought I understood what it meant to have a goal, a dream, a purpose in life. But then you came along, and everything I thought I knew changed.

You have been my second chance, my beginning, my future. Every time I look at you, I see a better version of myself, a hope I never knew I had.

I hope that one day, even for just a moment, you can feel the love I have for you.

I WOULD LIKE TO TELL YOU ABOUT THAT TIME WHEN I TALKED ABOUT YOU WITH SOMEONE, FULL OF EMOTION.

When the world
seems confused and
chaotic, all I have to
do is look at you to
find my balance.

You are my
compass, my
constant, my reason
for everything.

I WANT TO TELL YOU ABOUT THE TIME I CRIED, BUT
THEY WERE TEARS OF PURE JOY BECAUSE OF YOU.

I want you to know that you should never be afraid of making mistakes.

Life is full of difficult moments, mistakes, and choices that seem insurmountable.

But every mistake you make will bring you one step closer to who you are meant to be. You don't have to be perfect.

You don't always need to have all the answers. The only thing I want from you is to try.

To chase your dreams with all your heart, knowing that I will always be here, supporting you, believing in you, even in the moments when you don't believe in yourself.

I WANT TO TELL YOU WHAT STRUCK ME THE MOST
ABOUT THE WAY YOU ARE, FROM THE VERY FIRST DAY.

I remember the day I saw you for the
first time as if it were yesterday.
There was nothing in the world that
could have prepared me for that
moment.

I was scared, I admit it. But then,
when I held you in my arms, the
world became silent.

And in that silence, I found a
promise: that I would do everything
possible to protect you, to love you, to
teach you to believe in yourself.

I don't know if I did everything the
right way, but I know one thing: I
gave all of myself. And I would do it
again, and again, without hesitation.

I WANT TO TELL YOU WHICH ARE THE MEMORIES I HOLD MOST DEARLY IN MY HEART, MOMENTS THAT ARE ABOUT US.

I wish that one day you could see yourself through my eyes.

You would see an extraordinary person, full of potential, kindness, and strength.

You would see how much you are worth, how capable you are, and how much love there is inside you.

When I look at you, I don't just see the present; I see all the wonderful things you will do, all the lives you will touch, all the happiness you deserve.

Never forget that your worth doesn't depend on what you do, but on who you are.

And you, simply, are amazing.

I WOULD LIKE TO TELL YOU WHAT THE MOST
BEAUTIFUL GIFT YOU'VE EVER GIVEN ME IS.

If I could stop time, I would.

Not because I don't want to see
you grow, but because every
moment with you is a treasure
I want to keep with me forever.

Every laugh of yours, every hug,
every sweet word you say to me
are like little fragments of
happiness I keep in my heart.

I know that time can't be
stopped, and that one day you
will fly away to follow your
dreams.

But know that, wherever you
go, you will carry a part of me
with you.

I WANT TO TELL YOU HOW SURPRISED I WAS BY ONE
OF YOUR SPONTANEOUS ACTS OF KINDNESS.

My love for you is unconditional.

And to me, you are everything the world could have ever given me.

I WANT TO TELL YOU WHAT YOU LOVED TO DO
WHEN YOU WERE LITTLE.

There are days when I wonder if I have done enough.

If I've given you enough time, enough love, enough support.

But then I look at you, and I see a person growing with strength, kindness, and heart.

And I realize that, even though I'm not perfect, I must have done something right.

Because you are my greatest pride.

I WANT TO SHARE THIS DREAM WITH YOU.

No matter how big you get,
or how many things you
conquer in your life, in my
eyes, you will always be that
child who sought my hand in
moments of fear.

And I will always be here,
even when you think you
don't need me.

You will always be my little
miracle, my heart.

I WANT TO SHARE THIS THOUGHT WITH YOU.

If I close my eyes and think of you, I think of your smile.

The one that lights up everything, that melts away every fear, that makes any day better.

That smile is my strength in the hardest moments, my safe haven when I feel lost. I don't know if you'll ever understand how much it has meant to me.

But I want you to know that your smile, so simple and pure, is my daily miracle.

I WANT YOU TO KNOW SOMETHING THAT I'VE
NEVER TOLD YOU.

I want you to know how
much you've changed me.

Before you, I thought I
knew who I was, that I had
everything under control.
Then you came, and my
world turned upside down.

You taught me to see with
new eyes, to slow down
when everything was
moving too fast, to marvel
at the simplest things.

You taught me that love
means accepting, learning,
growing together.

You are not just a part of
me; you are the part I didn't
even know I was missing.

I WANT TO TELL YOU HOW I FELT THE FIRST TIME
YOU ACHIEVED ONE OF YOUR GOALS.

I want you to know how
difficult it was for me to let
you go for the first time.

The first time I saw you
take those first steps toward
independence, a part of my
heart broke.
But it was a beautiful pain,
the kind that makes you
proud.

Because in that moment, I
realized I was doing the
right thing: I was teaching
you to walk on your own,
even though my instinct
wanted to protect you
forever.

And I would do it again,
every time, because your
courage deserves to be free.

I WOULD LIKE YOU TO LEARN THIS FROM ME:

There are things I've never told you, maybe because I didn't know how.

Like the fact that sometimes I was afraid of making mistakes, of letting you down, of not being enough. But every time I felt that way, all I had to do was look at you.

Just seeing you grow with the heart you have, with the strength and sweetness that define you, made me realize that everything I did in my life led to you.

You are my greatest certainty, even in my moments of doubt.

I WOULD LIKE TO TELL YOU WHAT I DIDN'T EXPECT TO LEARN FROM THE EXPERIENCE OF BEING A PARENT.

One day, I will tell you
about all the sacrifices I
made for you.

Not because I want you to
feel indebted, but because I
want you to know that every
single choice was made with
love.

Every sacrifice, every
struggle, every sleepless
night was a way of saying to
you, 'I love you.' And I would
do it all over again, a
thousand times, without
hesitation.

Because seeing you happy is
the greatest reward life
could ever give me.

I WANT YOU TO ALWAYS REMEMBER THIS:

I hope that one day
you'll understand
the pride I feel every
time I see you face
the world.

Every small victory,
every time you
overcome a fear or
chase a dream, feels
like a victory for me
too.

No matter how far
you go or how many
times you fall,
knowing that you
try, that you put
your heart into
everything you do,
makes me the
happiest person in
the world.

You are my greatest
inspiration.

I WOULD LIKE TO TELL YOU WHAT I FEEL EVERY TIME I LOOK AT A PICTURE OF YOU WHEN YOU WERE LITTLE.

I remember the first time I heard
your laugh.

It was like a melody I had never
heard before, and one I hope to
hear for the rest of my life.

From that moment on, I
promised myself that I would do
everything possible to protect
that laugh, to make sure it would
always be a part of your world.

Never stop laughing, because in
that sound lies the purest beauty
I have ever known.

I WOULD LIKE TO TELL YOU WHAT IT MEANS TO ME TO HUG YOU.

I would like you to understand one day how much you have made me strong.

It wasn't something I expected, but loving you gave me a strength I didn't know I had.

You taught me never to give up, to fight for what matters, to not be afraid to show my emotions.

You have been my teacher, even though you may not know it, and for that, I will always be grateful.

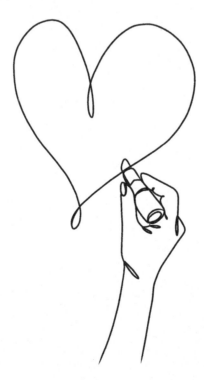

I WOULD LIKE TO TELL YOU ABOUT THAT BIRTHDAY OF YOURS WHEN...

I would like you to
know that, even on the
toughest days, you have
always been my light.

There have been
moments when
everything seemed to go
wrong, when worries
weighed on me like
heavy stones.

But then there was you,
with your way of making
everything simpler,
lighter.
You are my daily
reminder that, despite
everything, life is full of
wonder.

Never forget that, even
when you grow up.

I WOULD LIKE TO TELL YOU ABOUT ME AT YOUR AGE, HOW WE WERE ALIKE AND HOW WE WERE DIFFERENT.

You are so different from the little bundle I held in my arms the day you were born.

Your hands, which once clung to mine with all the strength you had, are now bigger, more confident, ready to reach toward the future.

Your eyes, which once sought mine for comfort, now look far ahead, toward horizons I can't yet imagine.
And yet, despite the passing of time, there is one thing that will never change: the love I have for you. It's a love that has no age, that knows no boundaries.

It started the day I knew you existed, and it has grown with every smile, every word, every step you've taken toward life. To me, you'll always be that child running toward me with open arms, filling my days with laughter and wonder.

One day, perhaps time will make these moments feel distant. Perhaps you will be too busy living your life, chasing your dreams, building your world. But I want you to always remember this: my love for you is eternal. No matter where life takes you, no matter how many changes we go through.

When you need to come back home, I will be here. Always.

I WOULD LIKE TO TELL YOU ABOUT THE DAY YOU LEARNED TO...

One day, I will tell you about all the times I doubted myself, but never you.

There were moments when I questioned whether I was doing enough, whether I was making the right decisions.

But when I looked at you, every doubt faded away. Because you are my greatest certainty, my most beautiful achievement.

No matter how many challenges you face, I know you will overcome them all, because within you is a strength that nothing and no one will ever extinguish.

I WANT TO PASS DOWN TO YOU THIS MEMORY OF YOUR GRANDPARENTS...

I treasure every gesture
of yours, every smile,
every glance like a
precious treasure.

It is these fragments of
life, the smallest ones
and perhaps the least
noticeable, that carry
with them all the magic
of being your parent.

I WOULD LIKE TO TELL YOU WHAT IT MEANS TO ME
TODAY TO BE A PARENT.

Some of the most beautiful
moments we've shared didn't need
words. There were no promises, no
speeches.

Just the beating of our hearts and
that sense of peace only you can
give me.

I want you to know that even in
the silences, there is love.
In the moments when it seems like
nothing is happening, there is
everything.

There is me, looking at you,
thinking about how important you
are, how you fill my life with
meaning.

Always remember this: you don't
need to make noise to feel how
much I love you.

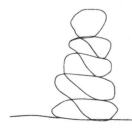

I WOULD LIKE TO TELL YOU AND REPEAT AGAIN AND AGAIN THAT...

There is something in you, something beyond words, a special way of being that I never wanted to change.

From the very first moment, I knew that you are not here to conform, to follow someone else's path. You are here to carve your own, and I have the privilege of watching you do so.

But know that it won't always be easy. There will be times when it feels like the world wants to change you, asks you to be something different from what you are. You'll look around and think you need to lower your voice, hide a part of yourself, to be accepted.

In those moments, I want you to remember this: you are enough. Just as you are. With your dreams, your passions, your fears.

Never stop being yourself, because it is your authenticity that makes you special, that makes the world more beautiful. My greatest wish is that you always have the courage to follow your heart.

Even when it's hard, even when it feels like no one understands. Because inside you is a light that must never be dimmed. Don't be afraid to shine. I will always be here to remind you how extraordinary you are, exactly as you are.

I WANT YOU TO READ THIS PAGE
WHEN YOU FEEL BLUE.

Every year, when Christmas arrives, my heart fills with a special joy.

I remember how we would wait together for Christmas Eve, with your eyes full of wonder and your laughter filling the house.

There was something magical in the air, as if everything stopped for a moment and we were the stars of a never-ending fairytale.

I want you to know that for me, those moments were the most precious. Seeing your happiness, your excitement while unwrapping gifts, decorating the tree, made me realize that the real gifts aren't the ones under the tree, but the moments we share.

Every Christmas spent together is a memory I treasure in my heart, a treasure that grows with you.

And even when you are grown up and far away, Christmas will always carry the scent of those moments, those laughs, that magic that only we shared.

I WANT TO SHARE THIS MEMORY WITH YOU.

There are days when I still feel your presence, small and perfect, in my womb.

You were there, hidden in a world that only we knew, yet already so alive, so mine.

Every movement, every beat of your heart, was a promise of a love that would become infinite.

There were no words, only feelings: the dream of seeing you, of holding you, of hearing your voice.

But even though I couldn't see you yet, I knew you were there, already loving me in a way that only you and I knew. You were my waiting, my happiness, my future.

I WANT TO TELL YOU THAT I FEEL HAPPY WHEN...

In this strange life, where everything seems to change in an instant, there is one thing I know for sure: nothing, absolutely nothing, will ever break the bond that unites us.

The roads we walk, the challenges we face, the difficult moments and the happy ones... every step will be a piece that enriches our journey, but the thread that binds us will always be the same, invisible and indestructible.

I know life will take us far, and maybe the distances between us will grow, but you will always be with me. And I will always be with you, even in the quietest moments, in the unspoken dreams, in the memories that only we share.

I want you to know that, no matter what happens, our bond is eternal. It is something that goes beyond time, beyond difficulties, beyond any uncertainty.

We are a part of each other, and even when the world changes, even when circumstances shift, our love will remain steadfast.

Always.

I WANT TO TELL YOU THAT YOU WILL
ALWAYS BE MY CHILD.

Thank you so much

If you are reading these words, it means you've chosen to dive into the pages of this book.
I thank you deeply for sharing this emotional journey with me.
Your words, your emotions, and your thoughts are the lifeblood that give strength to mine.
Every review, every feedback, every share is a small gesture that fuels my desire to write and share.
If this book touched your heart,
I kindly ask you for the great favor of leaving a review on Amazon.
Your opinion is precious and will be a source of eternal gratitude for me.

Scan the qr code to
leave a review

Made in the USA
Monee, IL
15 July 2025

21202332R00069